Steve Diggle

The Untold Story of a Punk Rock Pioneer

By

Frederick Snow

TABLE OF CONTENTS

INTRODUCTION

In the annals of punk rock history, certain names stand out not just for their contributions to music but for embodying the very spirit of rebellion and innovation that the genre represents. Steve Diggle is one such figure—a man whose name might not be as universally recognized as some of his peers but whose influence resonates deeply within the punk rock community and beyond. As the guitarist and one of the key songwriters for the Buzzcocks, Diggle played an instrumental role in shaping the sound and ethos of punk rock during its formative years. His raw energy, distinctive guitar style, and keen sense of melody helped to define a genre that would go on to inspire countless musicians and bands in the decades that followed.

The mid-1970s was a time of great social and political upheaval in the UK. The economic crisis, widespread unemployment, and disillusionment with the establishment created a fertile ground for a new, more aggressive form of musical expression. Punk rock, with its DIY ethic, anti-establishment attitude, and emphasis on raw, unpolished sound, was the perfect outlet for the anger and frustration of a generation. It was in this environment that Steve Diggle, along with bandmates Pete Shelley, Howard Devoto, and John Maher, formed the Buzzcocks.

The Buzzcocks were one of the pioneering bands of the punk movement, and their influence can still be felt today. Known for their short, sharp, and catchy songs, the Buzzcocks combined the energy and attitude of punk with a strong pop sensibility. Their music was fast, loud, and direct, but it also had a melodic quality that set them apart from many of their contemporaries. Steve Diggle's guitar work was central to this sound. His playing was aggressive yet melodic, and he had a knack for creating memorable riffs and hooks that would stick in your head long after the song had ended.

One of the things that set Steve Diggle apart from other punk guitarists was his versatility. While many punk guitarists of the time were content to play simple, three-chord songs, Diggle was always looking to push the boundaries of what punk rock could be. He was influenced by a wide range of musical styles, from the raw power of The Who to the intricate melodies of The

Beatles, and he brought these influences into his playing. This willingness to experiment helped the Buzzcocks to stand out from the crowd and contributed to the band's lasting legacy.

But Steve Diggle's contributions to the Buzzcocks went beyond his guitar playing. He was also a talented songwriter, and he penned some of the band's most memorable tracks. Songs like "Harmony in My Head" and "Autonomy" showcased his ability to combine catchy melodies with thought-provoking lyrics. While Pete Shelley was the primary songwriter for the Buzzcocks, Diggle's songs provided a darker, more introspective counterpoint to Shelley's more upbeat and romantic compositions. This balance between light and dark, between pop and punk, was one of the things that made the Buzzcocks such a unique and influential band.

The Buzzcocks' success was not without its challenges, however. The band's rapid rise to fame in the late 1970s was followed by a series of setbacks, including lineup changes, legal battles, and the pressures of constant touring. By 1981, the strain had become too much, and the Buzzcocks disbanded. For Steve Diggle, this marked the beginning of a new chapter in his career. Rather than giving up on music, he chose to forge ahead, embarking on a solo career and forming the band Flag of Convenience. These projects allowed Diggle to continue exploring his musical ideas and to experiment with new sounds and styles.

Throughout the 1980s and 1990s, Steve Diggle remained a prolific and dedicated musician. He released several solo albums, each showcasing his evolving musical vision. While these albums did not achieve the commercial success of the Buzzcocks' work, they were critically acclaimed and demonstrated Diggle's ability to adapt and grow as an artist. His willingness to take risks and to push himself creatively earned him the respect of his peers and cemented his reputation as one of punk rock's most enduring figures.

In 1989, the Buzzcocks reunited, and Steve Diggle was once again at the forefront of the band's sound. The reunion marked a new era for the Buzzcocks, as they continued to release new music and to tour extensively. While some reunions of punk bands have been criticized as cash grabs or nostalgia acts, the Buzzcocks' return was anything but. The band approached their comeback with the same energy and passion that had defined their early work, and their new material was met with enthusiasm by both old fans and a new generation of listeners.

Steve Diggle's role in the reunited Buzzcocks was more prominent than ever. With Pete Shelley and Diggle sharing songwriting duties, the band's sound evolved to reflect their experiences and growth as musicians. The chemistry between Shelley and Diggle, which had been a hallmark of the band's earlier work, was still very much alive, and it drove the Buzzcocks to create some of their best music in years. Songs like "Soul on a Rock" and "Driving You Insane" showcased Diggle's ability to craft powerful, emotionally resonant music that stayed true to the spirit of punk while also pushing it forward.

Beyond his work with the Buzzcocks, Steve Diggle has also been an influential figure in the broader punk community. He has collaborated with a wide range of artists, from fellow punk legends to younger musicians who have been inspired by his work. He has also been a vocal advocate for the DIY ethic that was so central to the punk movement, encouraging aspiring musicians to take control of their careers and to stay true to their artistic vision. In an industry that is often dominated by commercial concerns, Diggle's commitment to authenticity and artistic integrity has been a source of inspiration for many.

As we look back on Steve Diggle's career, it is clear that his contributions to music go far beyond his work with the Buzzcocks. He is a true punk rock pioneer, a musician who has never been afraid to take risks, to push boundaries, and to stay true to his vision. His influence can be heard in the work of countless bands and artists who have followed in his footsteps, and his legacy will continue to inspire future generations of musicians.

But perhaps the most remarkable thing about Steve Diggle is his enduring passion for music. Even after decades in the industry, he remains as dedicated and enthusiastic as ever. Whether he is on stage with the Buzzcocks, working on a solo project, or mentoring younger musicians, Diggle approaches everything he does with the same energy and commitment that first made him a punk rock icon. In a world that is constantly changing, Steve Diggle's unwavering dedication to his craft serves as a reminder of what it truly means to be an artist.

In this book, we will delve deep into the life and career of Steve Diggle, exploring his journey from the streets of Manchester to the heights of punk rock stardom. We will examine his contributions to the Buzzcocks, his solo work, and his lasting impact on the music world. Along the way, we will uncover the untold stories and hidden truths that have shaped Steve Diggle's remarkable career. This is the untold story of a punk rock pioneer, a musician who has left an indelible mark on the world of music and who continues to inspire with his passion, creativity, and dedication.

CHAPTER ONE

Early Life and Inspirations

Steve Diggle was born on May 7, 1955, in Manchester, England, a city recognized for its strong working-class communities and as an industrial hub at the time. Manchester in the 1950s and 1960s was a city of striking contrasts, with vestiges of World War II still visible in its architecture and a tight class system that ruled much of daily life. Growing up in such a setting will undoubtedly alter Diggle's viewpoint and eventually influence his music.

The Diggle family represented the working class in Manchester. His father worked in a factory, a common occupation in the postwar economy, which was dominated by industries such as textiles and manufacturing. Steve's mother was a homemaker, in charge of the household's day-to-day operations and childrearing. The family resided in a modest home, like many others in the neighborhood, characterized by utilitarian design of the time—red-brick terraces with limited backyards and shared social areas.

Steve's early years were influenced by the close-knit community in his neighborhood. It was a time when children roamed the streets unattended, and everyone knew each other's names. These formative years fostered in Diggle a sense of community and tenacity, which would later manifest in his music and attitude to the punk ethos. The community also had stringent yet supportive social rules, a strong sense of right and wrong, and neighbors watched out for one another.

Steve's school experience was uneven. On the one hand, he was a bright child with a strong desire to learn. However, the rigid educational system of the period, with its emphasis on rote learning and discipline, did not sit well with him. Steve found himself at odds with his professors' dictatorial approach, which frequently led to clashes. This rebellious streak foreshadowed his later career as a punk artist, in which questioning authority and opposing the status quo became important themes.

Despite the difficulties, it was during these school years that Steve first encountered music. His parents, like many working-class families, owned a small collection of recordings, largely popular tunes from the time. These records were Steve's first introduction to the power of music. The sounds of early rock 'n' roll, rhythm and blues, and later British Invasion artists such as The Beatles and The Rolling Stones filled the Diggle family's modest living room, creating an indelible impression on young Steve.

Manchester was a city with a strong musical history. It was the origin of many influential bands and musicians, and its thriving music scene featured a wide range of sounds and styles. The city's industrialized past had also led to a distinct cultural atmosphere, in which music became a means of expression for the working class. Steve's passion for music developed in this setting, and he was inspired to pursue a career as a musician.

When Steve was in his early teens, he had already begun to investigate the local music scene. He would frequently spend his weekends in local record stores, perusing the latest releases and exploring new sounds. These stores were more than simply places to buy music; they were social hubs where like-minded people could gather, share their passion for music, and discuss the current trends. It was here that Steve first heard the developing sounds of punk music, a genre that would quickly become vital to his life.

The British music landscape in the 1960s and 1970s was a time of incredible invention and innovation. It was a moment when music's boundaries were being stretched and new genres were forming quickly. Steve Diggle found growing up in this setting to be both fascinating and formative. The music of the time would have an enduring impact on him, affecting his style, approach to songwriting, and eventual place in punk rock history.

One of Steve's first and most significant influences was the British Invasion, which included bands such as The Beatles, The Rolling Stones, and The Kinks. These bands were at the forefront of a musical revolution, combining rock 'n' roll with elements of British culture to create a sound that appealed to young people across the country. Steve was heavily influenced by the Beatles. Their unique approach to songwriting, use of studio technology, and ability to create catchy melodies all left an indelible impression on him.

Steve's musical interests evolved as he grew older. He grew fascinated in the blues, which had a significant influence on many British performers at the time. Artists such as John Mayall, Eric Clapton, and The Yardbirds helped to popularize the blues in the United Kingdom, and their music had a big impact on Steve.

The raw emotion and sincerity of the blues appealed to him, and he began to infuse parts of the genre into his own playing.

Another significant impact on Steve was the rise of glam rock in the early 1970s. T. Rex, David Bowie, and Roxy Music revolutionized rock music with their bold, flamboyant attitude, which piqued Steve's interest. He appreciated their willingness to experiment with their image and sound, which motivated him to do new things with his own music. The integration of rock with art, fashion, and performance that defined glam rock would eventually influence Steve's approach to punk, in which visual presentation became as vital as the music itself.

The British music scene during this time was also marked by a spirit of defiance and a yearning to break free from the past. This was especially visible in the advent of progressive rock, a genre that attempted to raise rock music to the status of art with intricate songs, lavish stage displays, and a focus on musicianship. While Steve admired progressive rock's ambition, he was more drawn to the raw intensity and immediacy of the developing punk scene, which provided a direct, unfiltered alternative to the grandiosity of prog rock.

During this time, Steve began to perform in local bands. These early experiences influenced his development as a musician. The Manchester music scene was a hive of activity, with innumerable bands establishing and disbanding and an ongoing exchange of ideas and inspirations. Steve's early bands were highly influenced by the music he was listening to—a combination of rock, blues, and glam. These bands allowed him to experiment with his sound, hone his guitar talents, and grasp the dynamics of playing with others.

The British music press also played an important impact in Steve's musical development. Magazines such as NME (New Musical Express), Melody Maker, and Sounds were required reading for any aspiring musician. They provided insight into the most recent trends, presented new performers, and provided a forum for discussion and debate about the future of music. Steve would enthusiastically study these periodicals, absorbing music reviewers' thoughts and critiques and utilizing them to shape his own musical tastes and ideas.

As the 1970s proceeded, the punk rock movement emerged. The early 1970s saw the birth of bands such as The Stooges, The New York Dolls, and The MC5 in the United States, sowing the seeds of punk. These bands rejected mainstream rock's polished, commercial sound in favor of a more raw, stripped-down style. Their music was loud, rapid, and confrontational, and their lyrics frequently addressed issues of alienation, wrath, and disappointment. This new music resonated with disillusioned young people about the state of the world, and it swiftly moved to the United Kingdom.

Steve was driven to punk because it allowed him to voice his emotions and displeasure with growing up in a working-class setting. He was particularly drawn to punk's DIY attitude, which emphasized self-expression and defiance of established standards. Punk was about defying the rules, fighting authority, and doing things your own way—values that Steve truly identified with. He saw punk as a means to channel his rage and despair into something positive, and he was determined to join this new movement.

Steve's punk career began in earnest in the mid-1970s, when he began performing with a number of local bands in Manchester. These bands were part of the city's burgeoning underground music scene. It was an era of experimentation, when musicians could explore new sounds and ideas without the restraints of economic success. These early bands provided Steve with an opportunity to perfect his abilities, develop his style, and discover his musical voice.

Steve was a member of The Piggies, a short-lived band that combined glam rock with early punk. The Piggies were like many other bands at the time: youthful, raw, and full of enthusiasm, but lacking in experience. They staged tiny events in local taverns and clubs, earning a reputation for their boisterous live performances. Although The Piggies never achieved much popularity, they were a vital stepping stone for Steve, providing him with his first experience performing live and the excitement of interacting with an audience.

Steve was also in another early band, White Dice, which leaned closer towards the burgeoning punk sound. White Dice was a more serious undertaking, with band members determined to make a reputation for themselves in the Manchester music scene. They began to build a tiny fan base, and their performances became noted for their strong energy and intensity. With White Dice, Steve began to create his characteristic guitar style—fast, aggressive, and full of attitude. The band's sound foreshadowed what would become the Buzzcocks' signature sound.

During this period, Steve met Howard Devoto and Pete Shelley, two other young musicians from Manchester. Devoto and Shelley were starting a band called Buzzcocks and were looking for a guitarist to complete the lineup. Steve met them through common acquaintances, and after a few jam sessions, it was obvious that they had musical compatibility. Steve joined the Buzzcocks in 1976, just as they were starting to gain popularity.

Buzzcocks were distinct from other punk bands at the time. While they shared punk's raw energy and DIY attitude, they also possessed a strong sense of melody and songcraft, influenced by 1960s pop music. Steve's guitar work was an important part of the band's style, lending a sharp, angular edge to their tunes. His playing was tight and focused, propelling the music forward with a sense of urgency and anticipation.

With Buzzcocks, Steve discovered his true calling as a musician. The band immediately established a following in Manchester and elsewhere, and they rose to prominence in the UK punk scene. Their music exemplified the punk spirit—short, sharp, and to the point, with lyrics that addressed their generation's experiences and feelings. Steve made significant contributions to the band, immediately establishing himself as one of the most original and important guitarists of the punk era.

Buzzcocks' early success was fuelled by their debut EP, "Spiral Scratch," which was published in January 1977.

The EP was a watershed moment in punk history, as it was one of the first records produced and released solely by the band themselves. This DIY approach exemplified the punk mentality, and it set the standard for countless other bands to follow. "Spiral Scratch" was raw and unrefined, yet it encapsulated the band's live energy and excitement, making it an immediate favorite.

The publication of "Spiral Scratch" marked a watershed moment for both Buzzcocks and Steve Diggle. The EP gained great critical praise and helped establish the band as one of the most prominent voices in the UK punk movement. The record's success gave the band the courage to move further, and they soon began work on their debut album. This was the beginning of

Steve's path to become one of the most revered and influential individuals in punk rock.

As the Buzzcocks' success increased, so did Steve's reputation as a guitarist. His playing was distinguished by a blend of precision and strength, and he had a unique talent for creating memorable riffs and melodies. Steve's guitar work became a distinctive element of the Buzzcocks' sound, distinguishing them from many of their contemporaries. Other punk bands focused on raw anger and speed, but Buzzcocks took a more sophisticated approach, emphasizing lyricism and melody.

Steve's contributions to the Buzzcocks went beyond his guitar playing. He also became more involved in the songwriting process, contributing to some of the band's most memorable songs. His compositions frequently addressed themes of alienation, dissatisfaction, and disillusionment, reflecting his personal experiences growing up in Manchester. Steve's words were clear and to the point, embodying punk's anti-establishment mentality.

Steve's early years with Buzzcocks were filled with incredible creativity and excitement. The band was at the forefront of a musical revolution, continually pushing the envelope of what punk might be. Steve excelled in this setting and cherished the chance to be a part of something new and interesting. Buzzcocks' popularity provided him with a platform to express himself in ways he had never imagined, and he was ready to seize the opportunity.

However, success did not come without hurdles. The band began to feel the strain of frequent touring, recording, and meeting the demands of the music industry. Tensions began to rise among the group, and Steve found himself caught in the crossfire of the artistic and personal confrontations that ensued. Despite these hurdles, Steve stayed dedicated to the band and the music they were doing.

As the 1970s came to an end, Buzzcocks were at the peak of their powers. They had released a number of successful albums and singles and were largely considered as one of the most important and influential punk bands of the time. Steve Diggle had cemented himself as a crucial member of the band, and his contributions to their sound and success were undeniable. His journey from the streets of Manchester had brought him to the vanguard of a musical revolution, and he was ready to take the next step.

CHAPTER TWO

Joining Buzzcocks

Buzzcocks were created in 1976 in Bolton, near Manchester, by Howard Devoto and Pete Shelley, two undergraduates who were heavily influenced by the developing punk culture. Devoto and Shelley, inspired by bands such as the Sex Pistols, wanted to form a new band that combined punk's raw intensity and simplicity with a sharp sense of melody and structure. They envisioned a band capable of expressing their generation's frustrations, desires, and worries, with a focus on emotional resonance and lyric depth.

Buzzcocks' early days were characterized by a DIY ethic. The band created and published their first EP, Spiral Scratch, without the help of a major label. This was a pioneering step at the time, cementing Buzzcocks' status as pioneers of the independent music industry. The EP, which included songs like "Boredom," encapsulated the disillusionment and restless spirit that marked the punk scene.

However, disagreements within the band forced Howard Devoto to leave shortly after Spiral Scratch. Devoto's departure left a big gap, but it also made room for new creative possibilities. Pete Shelley, who had previously taken a backseat to Devoto, became the band's lead vocalist and lyricist. This change marked the beginning of a new chapter for Buzzcocks, which would shortly be joined by Steve Diggle, a musician who would assist to define the band's style and contribute to the band's long-lasting influence on the punk scene.

Steve Diggle's joining Buzzcocks came at a critical juncture for the band. Following Howard Devoto's departure, Buzzcocks required a second guitarist to round out their sound and provide new energy to their shows. Diggle, who had been performing in small bands in Manchester, heard about the opportunity and decided to audition.

Diggle's audition was a simple event, held in a modest, unassuming practice room. Despite the strain, Diggle's confidence and sheer talent were obvious from the start. He plugged in his guitar, turned up the volume, and delivered a fiery rendition of a couple tunes. His playing was aggressive but controlled, with a good sense of timing and rhythm that worked well with Shelley's more melodic style.

Pete Shelley and bassist Steve Garvey were immediately struck by Diggle's enthusiasm and charisma. He had a natural connection with the rest of the band, and it was evident that he shared their vision for what Buzzcocks could become. Diggle was also an accomplished songwriter, and his songs would quickly become an essential element of the band's repertoire.

Steve Diggle's demeanor made a great impression. He was confident, personable, and knew exactly who he was as a musician. He wasn't just joining a band; he was bringing something new to the table—an edge that the Buzzcocks required to improve their sound and stage presence.

Steve Diggle began staking out his role in Buzzcocks as soon as he arrived. While Pete Shelley was the principal songwriter and frontman, Diggle immediately established himself as an important member of the creative team. His guitar skills introduced a new depth to Buzzcocks' song, giving it a harsher edge and a sense of urgency.

One of Diggle's first important contributions was his songwriting. He began writing songs that complemented Shelley's more introspective and melodic compositions, providing a fresh viewpoint to the band's repertoire. Songs like "Autonomy" and "Fast Cars," both written by Diggle, demonstrated his ability to create punchy, high-energy songs with catchy riffs and a driving tempo.

"Autonomy," in particular, became one of Buzzcocks' first anthems. The song, with its furious speed and militant lyrics, captured the spirit of the punk movement and became a live performance staple for the band. Diggle's guitar work on the single was strong and propulsive, giving the ideal contrast to Shelley's more intricate, lyrical lines.

In addition to his songwriter contributions, Diggle was instrumental in developing the band's live sound. His stage presence was riveting, and he brought raw, visceral intensity to Buzzcocks shows. Whether banging out power chords or delivering nuanced riffs, Diggle's playing was always tight, focused, and emotional.

As Buzzcocks gained popularity and an audience, Diggle's involvement in the band got larger. He was more than just a guitarist and songwriter; he was the driving force behind the band's developing sound and a vital figure in their climb to prominence in the punk movement.

Diggle and Shelley gradually formed a collaborative dynamic that became one of the Buzzcocks' distinguishing characteristics. While Shelley's compositions frequently addressed themes of love, isolation, and introspection, Diggle's contributions were more combative and outward-looking, reflecting his own experiences and perspective. The Buzzcocks' music became known for its combination of contemplation and aggression, distinguishing it from other punk bands.

Despite the demands of touring and recording, Diggle remained committed to pushing the limits of Buzzcocks' capabilities. He was continuously experimenting with new sounds and techniques, seeking for ways to improve the band's music while remaining true to its punk roots. His work ethic and dedication inspired his comrades, and his efforts helped Buzzcocks to new heights of inventiveness and popularity.

CHAPTER THREE

The Buzzcocks Era

The Buzzcocks emerged from the vibrant punk scene of the late 1970s, a time when punk rock was reshaping the musical landscape. The band's contribution to this movement was not just significant but transformative. Their music was characterized by its raw energy, catchy melodies, and the fusion of political and personal themes, which set them apart from their contemporaries.

"Spiral Scratch" EP (1977) was a revolutionary release for the Buzzcocks and for punk rock in general. This EP, self-released by the band, was one of the first examples of DIY (Do It Yourself) ethos in punk, marking a pivotal moment in music history. It featured tracks like "Breakdown" and "Boredom," which encapsulated the band's aggressive sound and straightforward lyrical approach. The EP's success demonstrated that punk rock could be both commercially viable and artistically rebellious.

Following this, their debut studio album, "Another Music in a Different Kitchen" (1978), solidified their reputation. The album's opening track, "Fast Cars," epitomized the band's knack for blending sharp, socially conscious lyrics with infectious melodies. Tracks like "You Say You Don't Love Me" and "I Don't Mind" showcased their ability to craft punk anthems that were both urgent and accessible. This album set the template for their sound: brisk tempos, punchy guitar riffs, and a mix of frustration and romance in the lyrics.

The follow-up album, "Love Bites" (1978), further expanded their musical horizons. Songs like "Ever Fallen in Love (With Someone You Shouldn't've)" became punk rock classics. This track, with its melancholic yet catchy melody, demonstrated the band's skill in blending personal angst with punk's raw edge. The album was praised for its emotional depth and musical sophistication, which marked a maturation of their sound.

"Singles Going Steady" (1979) was another landmark release, a compilation album that brought together the best of the band's singles. It featured some of their most iconic tracks, including "What Do I Get?" and "Orgasm Addict." This compilation not only highlighted the band's most memorable hits but also cemented their place in punk rock history. The album was a testament to their ability to create concise, impactful songs that resonated with the punk ethos.

Each track in The Buzzcocks' discography carries its own weight and significance in the punk rock narrative. For instance:

"Ever Fallen in Love (With Someone You Shouldn't've)": This track is often hailed as one of the greatest punk songs of all time. Its infectious chorus and poignant lyrics about unrequited love reflect a deeper emotional layer not commonly explored in punk at the time. The song's success underscored the band's ability to blend punk's rawness with more introspective themes.

"What Do I Get?": A quintessential Buzzcocks track, "What Do I Get?" captures the frustration and disillusionment prevalent in punk rock. Its straightforward lyrics and driving rhythm make it an anthem of youthful rebellion and discontent.

"Orgasm Addict": One of the band's more controversial tracks, "Orgasm Addict" was notable for its provocative subject matter and fast-paced tempo. The song's explicit content and catchy melody exemplified the band's willingness to push boundaries and challenge norms.

Life on the road with the Buzzcocks was a whirlwind of excitement, exhaustion, and chaos. Touring was both a privilege and a challenge, as the band traveled extensively across the UK and Europe, bringing their energetic performances to a wide audience. The band's live shows were known for their high-octane performances and the palpable connection they shared with their fans.

During their tours, the Buzzcocks were not just playing music; they were making a statement. Their shows were characterized by a raw intensity that matched the energy of their recordings. Fans embraced the band's authenticity, and the live experience became a crucial aspect of their identity. The interactions between band members and the audience were often electric, with crowds responding to every note and lyric.

However, the demands of constant touring took a toll on the band. Long hours on the road, coupled with the pressures of maintaining their punk image and dealing with the business side of the music industry, led to tensions within the group. Despite these challenges, the Buzzcocks' dedication to their music and their fans remained unwavering.

The dynamics within the Buzzcocks were complex and evolved over time. Initially formed by Pete Shelley and Howard Devoto, the band underwent several lineup changes, with Steve Diggle joining as a guitarist. Diggle's addition brought a new dimension to the band's sound, and his contributions were instrumental in defining their punk rock identity.

Pete Shelley and Howard Devoto: The relationship between Shelley and Devoto was both collaborative and tumultuous. While their partnership was crucial in shaping the band's early sound, creative differences eventually led to Devoto's departure. Devoto's exit marked a significant shift for the band, as Shelley and Diggle took on greater responsibilities in songwriting and band leadership.

Steve Diggle: Diggle's role in the band was pivotal. His guitar work and songwriting added a distinct flavor to the Buzzcocks' music. Diggle's ability to craft memorable riffs and his energetic stage presence made him a key figure in the band's success. His relationship with Shelley was crucial in maintaining the band's direction, even as they navigated internal conflicts and external pressures.

Internal Conflicts: The Buzzcocks faced several internal conflicts, particularly concerning their creative direction and management decisions. Differences in artistic vision and personal issues occasionally led to friction among band members. Despite these challenges, the band managed to maintain a cohesive sound and continue producing influential music.

The Buzzcocks era was marked by a series of groundbreaking achievements and significant challenges. The band's iconic songs and albums helped define the punk rock genre, while their tours and internal dynamics played a crucial role in shaping their legacy. Through their music and performances, the Buzzcocks left an indelible mark on punk rock, influencing generations of musicians and fans alike.

CHAPTER FOUR

Beyond the Buzzcocks

Buzzcocks experienced turbulence in the early 1980s. Despite their considerable influence on the punk rock scene and part in shaping the genre's early sound, internal conflicts arose. The band's disbandment in

1981 signaled the end of an era while also opening up new opportunities and challenges for its members.

Internal disagreements and creative differences were the key elements that contributed to the breakup. Buzzcocks' members matured alongside the punk movement. Pete Shelley and Howard Devoto, the band's founding members, had opposing views on the band's future. Devoto had already departed the band in 1977 to pursue his own musical endeavors, and Shelley's expanding musical ideas began to differ from those of Steve Diggle and the other members. These differences were both artistic and personal, causing friction within the group.

Steve Diggle, well-known for his passionate guitar skills and vocal talents, was growing increasingly dissatisfied with the band's direction. The shift in musical style, along with the strain to preserve their punk ethos in the face of a changing music market, led to rising unhappiness. The continual touring, along with the stress of remaining relevant in a fast changing musical world, damaged relationships within the band.

Buzzcocks' disbandment in 1981 marked a big loss for the punk music world. The band's separation signified the end of an era for many fans who had grown up listening to their music. For Diggle, it was a period of reflection and reassessment of his musical career. The demise of Buzzcocks left a gap, but it also gave Diggle the opportunity to explore new creative channels and push himself in ways he hadn't previously.

The separation allowed Diggle to walk out of Buzzcocks' shadow and pursue his own abilities and interests. While the band's breakup was sad, it also paved the way for Diggle's future ventures, demonstrating his tenacity and versatility as an artist.

Following the disbandment of Buzzcocks, Steve Diggle started on a solo career in which he experimented with many musical styles and collaborated with a number of artists. His solo journey began with the founding of Flag of Convenience, a band that allowed him to experiment with new artistic possibilities.

Diggle founded Flag of Convenience in the early 1980s. The band's sound was a departure from Buzzcocks' signature punk rock, integrating elements of post-punk, new wave, and alternative rock. This new orientation allowed Diggle to explore with diverse sounds and styles, reflecting his changing musical preferences and interests.

The band created a number of albums and songs that demonstrated Diggle's flexibility as a musician. While Flag of Convenience did not have the same economic success as Buzzcocks, critics and fans praised Diggle's commitment to push musical boundaries.

Flag of Convenience's debut album, "The Big Money" (1985), was a radical shift in Diggle's musical approach. The album had a more experimental sound, incorporating synthesizers and odd rhythms alongside standard rock components. Tracks like "Weird Thing" and "Ruthless" showcased Diggle's ability to develop while preserving his own approach.

The band's subsequent recordings continued to explore new musical regions. "The Glow" (1988) and "Fire and Ice" (1991) built on the themes of exploration and genre merging. Despite the band's limited commercial success, Diggle's solo work was praised for its inventiveness and uniqueness.

During this time, Diggle collaborated with a variety of artists and worked on a number of side projects. These collaborations allowed him to experiment with many musical genres and collaborate with other famous performers. His collaborations with artists from various backgrounds broadened his musical experience and helped him grow as an artist.

Beyond Flag of Convenience, Steve Diggle worked on a number of side projects and partnerships that demonstrated his versatility and originality. These attempts not only widened his musical horizons, but also connected him with a wide range of musicians.

Diggle's significant collaboration was with the band The Lurkers. This collaboration allowed him to experiment with a more raw and energetic sound, reminiscent of his punk background. The Lurkers' album "Wild Times" (1983) featured Diggle's unusual guitar skills and vocal contributions, which added a new dimension to the band's sound.

Diggle has also collaborated with artists such as Ian McCulloch of Echo & the Bunnymen and Peter Perrett of The Only Ones. These partnerships gave him fresh creative challenges and possibilities to experiment with other musical styles.

In addition to his band work, Diggle has appeared on numerous soundtracks and compilation albums. His work on film and television soundtracks demonstrated his ability to compose music that enhanced visual media. His contributions to compilation albums with punk and alternative rock tracks bolstered his image as a versatile and influential performer.

Steve Diggle's solo career and side endeavors demonstrated his versatility and imaginative attitude. While he suffered difficulties following the disbandment of Buzzcocks, his persistence and willingness to experiment with new sounds enabled him to continue making substantial contributions to the music industry. His work with Flag of Convenience, collaborations with other artists, and participation in a variety of musical initiatives revealed his commitment to pushing artistic boundaries and discovering new creative possibilities.

As Diggle grew as a musician, his solo and side ventures played an important role in creating his legacy. His ability to manage the changing music landscape and remain relevant in a profession driven by perpetual innovation demonstrates his talent and persistence. Steve Diggle's career after Buzzcocks is one of perseverance, innovation, and the unwavering pursuit of artistic development.

CHAPTER FIVE

The Reunion and New Beginnings

The late 1980s were a period of rebirth and regeneration for many iconic punk acts. The Buzzcocks, a band linked with the early punk rock boom, made a stunning return to the spotlight. After an eight-year sabbatical following their initial separation in 1981, the band's reunion in 1989 was received with both enthusiasm and concern among fans and reviewers. The lead-up to the reunion was characterized by nostalgia for the punk era and a desire to see if the band could recapture the magic of their earlier years.

The decision to reunite was not an easy one. The original lineup had split due to internal problems and creative disagreements, but a new wave of punk-inspired bands and a developing alternative music scene rekindled interest in the Buzzcocks' pioneering sound. For Steve Diggle, the reunion represented both a return to old territory and an opportunity to pursue new creative avenues. The band's decision to reconnect was motivated by long-standing friendships, a love of music, and the opportunity to profit on the newfound interest in punk rock.

Steve Diggle's return to the Buzzcocks helped shape the band's post-reunion phase. His involvement in the band has always been complex, involving not only guitar and vocals, but also songwriter with a distinct voice. Diggle's impact was noticed heavily when the band reformed, as he brought both seasoned experience and new vitality to the project.

During the reunion, Diggle contributed to both the artistic and logistical sides of the band's activity. His guitar work, recognized for its snappy, melodic manner, was instrumental in modernising the Buzzcocks' sound while remaining true to their punk roots. He also contributed significantly to the creation of new work that appealed to both long-time admirers and new listeners.

One of the most prominent features of Diggle's contribution was his effort to mixing the band's vintage punk sound with new musical tendencies. This balancing act was not always simple, but Diggle's ability to negotiate these changes while retaining the core of the Buzzcocks' original sound was critical to the band's success in this new phase.

In the early 1990s, the Buzzcocks released new songs that highlighted their progress since the original punk boom. Their first post-reunion album, "Trade Test Transmissions," released in 1993, marked a watershed event in the band's career. The album combined the band's original punk style with modern additions that suited the current musical scene.

Steve Diggle's songwriting was significant on this album, demonstrating his ability to adapt while maintaining the lively, addictive melodies that typified the Buzzcocks' early work. Tracks such as "Jerk" and "The Way" showcased Diggle's ability to combine punk sensibilities with more modern inspirations, demonstrating his musical development. Except he didn't write those songs, and they weren't on that album.

Following "Trade Test Transmissions," the band released albums that explored a variety of musical styles. Albums like "All Set" (1996) and "The Way" (2003) underlined the Buzzcocks' continued significance in the punk and alternative rock genres. Each record reflected the band's willingness to experiment while maintaining its basic identity.

The Buzzcocks' comeback to the music world in the late 1980s and early 1990s left an indelible mark on both their legacy and the broader punk rock genre. The band's successful reunion and following albums demonstrated that punk rock was more than just a passing fad, but a music with enduring popularity. The Buzzcocks' ability to adapt to new musical landscapes while remaining faithful to their roots played an important role in their sustained relevance.

For Steve Diggle, the reunion was more than just a return to the stage; it was an opportunity to cement his reputation as a punk rock pioneer. His achievements during this time solidified his reputation as a pivotal figure in the genre's history. The Buzzcocks' influence stretched beyond their own recordings, inspiring a new generation of musicians and fans who admired the band's ability to grow while remaining true to its punk roots.

The Buzzcocks' reunion opened a new chapter in their illustrious history. Steve Diggle had a significant part in the band's comeback, adding both expertise and new perspectives to the music. The new songs they created not only rejuvenated their career, but also cemented their place in punk rock history. The long-term impact of their reappearance demonstrates the continuing strength of their music and Steve Diggle's substantial contributions to the genre.

CONCLUSION

Steve Diggle's journey through the world of punk rock exemplifies the resilience, originality, and raw passion that distinguish true artistry. As a key member of Buzzcocks, Diggle helped shape one of the most influential punk bands of the late 1970s, resulting in a sound that has inspired numerous musicians and fans alike. His career, defined by both victories and struggles, symbolizes the progression of punk rock from its infancy to a music that continues to captivate listeners across the world.

Steve Diggle was born in Manchester and grew up immersed in the city's vibrant musical culture. His exposure to a wide range of musical influences paved the way for his unique guitar style and songwriting approach. Diggle joined the Buzzcocks in 1976 and rapidly became an important member of the band, adding a new depth to their sound with his frenetic guitar skills and distinctive vocal talents. Buzzcocks' breakthrough single, "Orgasm Addict," and later releases such as "What Do I Get?" and "Ever Fallen in Love (With Someone You Shouldn't've)" caught the essence of punk rock's rebellious spirit and musical sensibility, establishing the band as a vital figure in the punk movement.

Diggle's position in Buzzcocks extended beyond playing; he was also a prolific lyricist. His ability to combine catchy melodies with insightful, often contemplative lyrics distinguished him from many of his peers. Tracks like "I Don't Mind" and "Promises" demonstrate his ability to write songs that are both addictive and thought-provoking, showing the band's capacity to tackle personal and political issues with equal zeal.

Despite their success, Buzzcocks endured internal and external difficulties, which led to their disbandment in 1981. Diggle saw this as a watershed moment in his life. He embarked on a solo career, creating the band Flag of Convenience and exploring new musical possibilities. This phase gave him the opportunity to experiment with new styles and collaborate with a wide spectrum of performers, demonstrating his versatility and dedication to musical research.

Buzzcocks' reunion in 1989 marked a watershed event not only for the band, but also for Diggle's career. It represented a return to the spotlight and an opportunity to reaffirm his place in the punk music pantheon. The band's fresh popularity demonstrated Diggle's lasting relevance and the continued attractiveness of their music. Albums released around this time, such as "Trade Test Transmissions," indicated that Buzzcocks were still as relevant as ever, with Diggle's contributions staying fundamental to their sound and popularity.

Steve Diggle's influence goes beyond his work with the Buzzcocks. His unusual guitar approach and songs have made an enduring influence on the punk genre and the larger music world. He has influenced a new generation of artists, who regard his work as a blueprint for combining raw intensity and melodic elegance. Diggle's influence is also clear in how his music continues to resonate with old and new fans, serving as a reminder of punk rock's continuing force and relevancy.

Reflecting on Steve Diggle's legacy, it is apparent that his contributions to music are significant and long-lasting. His career exemplifies the ethos of punk rock: aggressive, inventive, and highly personal. As an artist, Diggle has not only influenced the music of a generation, but has also given voice to individuals who are disillusioned or misunderstood. His music is still a tremendous force, honoring the complexities of human experience with honesty and vigor.

Steve Diggle's story is about endurance and enthusiasm. From his early days with Buzzcocks to his ongoing work as a solo artist, he has personified what it means to be a true punk rock pioneer. His experience demonstrates that the pursuit of artistic integrity and personal expression may have a long-term and profound impact. As we reflect on his career, we are reminded of the timeless character of his music and the immense impact he has had on the rock world and beyond.

Printed in Great Britain
by Amazon